MUSICAL GENIUS

A Creative Minds Biography

MUSICAL GENIUS

A Story about
Wolfgang Amadeus Mozart

by Barbara Allman

illustrations by Janet Hamlin

 Carolrhoda Books, Inc./Minneapolis

For my mother, who sang to me,
and my father, who danced with me
— *B. A.*

This book is available in two editions:
Library binding by Carolrhoda Books, Inc.,
    a division of Lerner Publishing Group
Soft cover by First Avenue Editions,
    an imprint of Lerner Publishing Group
241 First Avenue North
Minneapolis, MN 55401 U.S.A.

Website address: www.lernerbooks.com

Library of Congress Cataloging-in-Publication Data

Allman, Barbara.
    Musical genius : a story about Wolfgang Amadeus Mozart / by Barbara
Allman ; illustrations by Janet Hamlin.
        p.   cm. — (A creative minds biography)
    Summary: Describes the life of eighteenth-century Austrian composer,
Mozart, a musical prodigy who learned to write music before he could
write letters and grew up to become Imperial Court Composer to Emperor
Joseph.
    Includes bibliographical references and index.
    ISBN: 1–57505–604–6 (lib. bdg. : alk. paper)
    ISBN: 1–57505–637–2 (pbk. : alk. paper)
    1. Mozart, Wolfgang Amadeus, 1756–1791—Juvenile literature.
2. Composers—Austria—Biography—Juvenile literature. [1. Mozart,
Wolfgang Amadeus, 1756–1791. 2. Composers.] I. Hamlin, Janet, ill.
II. Title. III. Series.
ML3930.M9A45 2004
780'.92—dc22   2003015088

Manufactured in the United States of America
1 2 3 4 5 6 – JR – 09 08 07 06 05 04

Table of Contents

1

Wonder Child

Three-year-old Wolfgang sat on the floor with his toys, listening. His older sister, Maria Anna, was having her music lesson from Papa at the keyboard. Only eight years old, she played remarkably well. Music delighted Wolfgang, and something inside of him yearned to make music too. When Nannerl (the family's name for Maria Anna) and Papa finished the lesson, Wolfgang scurried over to the keyboard. Reaching up to the keys, the blond-haired little boy plinked out sounds that pleased his ear. Wolfgang was already on his way to making music.

Wolfgang had been born in Salzburg, in the Holy Roman Empire, to Anna Maria and Leopold Mozart on January 27, 1756. It had been a bitterly cold Sunday. Not much was known in those days about how to prevent sickness in babies. Five of the Mozarts' babies had not lived long. They hoped their seventh child would be blessed. So the very next day, he was tenderly bundled up and taken to the cathedral to be baptized. The tiny child was given the very long name Joannes Chrysostomus Wolfgangus Theophilus Mozart. (Theophilus meant "loved by God" in Greek. It was Amadeus in Latin.) Most of the time, his family called him Wolfgang after his grandfather.

Wolfgang lived with his mother, father, and sister, their dog, and a favorite pet canary. The family lived on the fourth floor of a comfortable five-story apartment house in the city. Papa did not have far to walk to work. He was a musician at the royal court of Salzburg and worked for Archbishop Schrattenbach. The archbishop was one of the many archbishops, electors, and princes who ruled small German and Austrian states in the Holy Roman Empire. Leopold played the violin in the orchestra, wrote music for the church, and taught the choirboys to play the violin. The year that Wolfgang was born, his father published a book on violin playing. It became known far and wide for its good advice and solid teachings. Papa worked hard but he hadn't gotten the job he wanted most—kapellmeister—head of the orchestra.

Wolfgang's mother, Anna Maria, came from a musical family. She made a good home for her family, and she loved to laugh. In her younger days, she and Papa were known as the handsomest couple in Salzburg.

Four-year-old Wolfgang was proud to be using his big sister's musical notebook. Papa had put musical pieces into a notebook for Nannerl when she began learning to play. It was Wolfgang's turn to use it. The easiest pieces were at the beginning. Then they grew more difficult. Wolfgang was learning very quickly to play them all. Sometimes it seemed as if he already knew the things his father tried to teach him.

One afternoon, Wolfgang sat at the big desk in the drawing room, scratching on music paper with quill and ink. He was doing his best to write down the music he heard in his head. But he didn't quite know how to make the pen cooperate. There was a good deal of ink on the paper and on him.

Before long, Wolfgang heard Papa arrive home from work and climb the apartment stairs. Johann Schachtner, a trumpeter and violinist, came with him. Wolfgang, spattered with ink, looked up from Papa's desk. Papa asked him what he thought he was doing. The little boy told his father that he was writing a concerto. Instead of scolding Wolfgang for making a mess, Leopold asked to see his work. Papa and Herr Schachtner gave each other amused looks. Then they looked at the papers. They were amazed to see that Wolfgang had written musical notes. With tears in his eyes, Leopold praised his little son, telling him his concerto was very difficult to play.

Wolfgang replied that of course it was hard—that's what made it a concerto. "You must practice it until you get it right," stated Wolfgang. Then as best as he could with his small hands on the keys, he showed Papa and Herr Schachtner how it went.

Leopold knew his children were gifted musicians, but Wolfgang astonished him. The boy could write musical notes, though he had not yet learned to write the letters of the alphabet.

One day Wolfgang discovered something that caught his interest almost as much as music—mathematics. Mathematics was orderly and logical like music. Also like music, there was something magical about it. For a while, Wolfgang tested Nannerl's patience with his talk of nothing but numbers. Before long, he was using the walls of the staircase as a chalkboard and writing numbers on them. Wolfgang was so interested in math that he wrote on the walls of all the rooms in the apartment. It took many a scolding from Mama before Wolfgang stopped writing on the walls.

Papa's friends often met to play music together at the Mozarts' home. One evening when Wolfgang was five, a group gathered to play some new music for stringed instruments—violins, violas, and cellos. Eagerly, Wolfgang got out his new child-sized violin. He asked Papa to allow him to play the second violin part. But Papa refused, telling him he could not play with the grown-ups. He had not begun his violin lessons yet. As Wolfgang turned away, he insisted he didn't need lessons to play second violin.

Herr Schachtner persuaded Leopold to let the little boy play along with him on the second violin part. The music began. Before long, Herr Schachtner realized that Wolfgang really could play the part. He quietly put down his violin and let Wolfgang finish playing. It was time for Papa to give Wolfgang violin lessons.

Wolfgang didn't know that his father was planning a trip to Munich, where he and Nannerl would play for royalty. Papa wanted people to see them as musical wonders—child geniuses. For now, life at home went on as usual. Wolfgang was taught to obey Papa. Every evening he stood dutifully on a chair. He and Papa took turns singing a little tune. "Oragna fiagata fa, marina gamina fa," Wolfgang sang out the nonsense words. Then he kissed Papa goodnight, hopped down from the chair, and danced off to bed.

2

Golden Years

Wolfgang listened to the plop-plop of the Danube waters lapping at the riverboat that had carried him and his family to Vienna. The six-year-old boy took in the sounds of the bustling docks. It was early October 1762. Wolfgang watched as the family's bags were deposited beside the canal along with sacks of mail and crates of goods. Customs inspectors began checking everyone's luggage. Here was an opportunity for Wolfgang. Papa took out the violin and urged Wolfgang to play. The boy had gotten used to playing for people on his trip to Munich. He loved the attention and didn't mind showing off, so he began to play. His fellow travelers were enchanted. Even the busy workers paused to listen to the "wonder child."

People talked about the little boy with the amazing musical talent. Within days, the musical Mozarts were invited to the palace to play for the royal family. Wolfgang was presented to Maria Theresa, the empress of the Holy Roman Empire. He showed her the same warmth he showed other people. He climbed onto her lap and gave her a hug and kiss. The motherly empress had many children of her own, and she was delighted with Wolfgang's greeting.

The children were invited back to the palace many times. Wolfgang enjoyed playing duets with his sister for the royal family. One day he was about to play some music by Herr Wagenseil, a famous court composer. Wolfgang asked the composer to sit next to him while he played. Then the little boy ordered the distinguished man to turn the pages of the music for him!

Wolfgang liked to play games with the royal children. One day they were playing in a palace hall. Wolfgang slipped and fell on the polished floor. One of the empress's children, seven-year-old Marie Antoinette, helped him back onto his feet. Grateful for her kindness, Wolfgang promised to marry the little archduchess when he grew up.

Wolfgang and Nannerl were very busy in Vienna. They were often invited to perform in the grand houses of wealthy people. In one day, Wolfgang performed at one home from half past two until quarter to four. Then he hopped into a carriage and went to play at another until half past five. Next, he went to the home of a count until nine o'clock.

Wolfgang shone during these visits. He sight-read music he had never seen before. He played the clavier—a keyboard instrument. He also improvised—he made up the music as he went along.

Wolfgang delighted people with his musical tricks. Sometimes he played the clavier with the keys covered by a cloth. When a clock chimed or a bell rang, he named the note perfectly. Wolfgang enjoyed making music so much that he really didn't mind performing all the time. Still, it was tiring work for someone so young.

The empress sent Nannerl and Wolfgang each an outfit that had been made for her own children. Papa had their portraits painted with Nannerl wearing her beautiful white brocade dress and Wolfgang in his handsome lilac blue suit with gold braided trim.

One day, after returning from the palace, Wolfgang wasn't feeling well. He grew sicker and sicker. He had caught scarlet fever. Four weeks passed before he recovered.

Wolfgang and his family left Vienna and headed for home. Once home, Papa began to plan for the next trip. Traveling was difficult in those days. Roads were muddy and bumpy. Wolfgang's father arranged for a private coach pulled by horses. It would be more comfortable than traveling in a public coach with strangers. Papa wanted to keep up appearances. After all, the Mozarts were going to Paris, France! It was the first time Wolfgang would travel outside the Holy Roman Empire.

Wolfgang and his family left Salzburg for Paris in June 1763. Not forty miles from home, Wolfgang suddenly felt a big bump and heard a clatter. A wheel had broken, and the coach almost rolled over. Luckily, no one was hurt. But it would take awhile for repairs. So Papa took Wolfgang to the local church to teach him how to use the pedals of the church organ. By pushing the pedals with his feet, Wolfgang could play the lowest notes. The seven-year-old boy learned quickly, though he had to stand up to reach the pedals.

There were many stops along the route to Paris. Wolfgang and his sister played for the nobility of whatever city they were in. They stayed in Augsburg to visit relatives and friends. When they left, they took along a portable clavier made by Papa's friend Johann Andreas Stein. Wolfgang could practice on it wherever they went.

The Mannheim Orchestra was in the town of Schwetzingen for the summer. There, Wolfgang was thrilled to hear the famous orchestra for the first time. He met some of the orchestra musicians and played for them as well. In the city of Frankfurt, the children gave a concert that was open to the public. Public concerts were still uncommon in those days in much of Europe. Most musicians worked for orchestras supported by the nobility. They gave private concerts. Composers wrote music commissioned by the upper class.

The Mozarts' summer journey continued into fall. Wolfgang and his family went to the cities of Bonn, Cologne, and Brussels. In many places, Wolfgang and Nannerl were admired and honored with gifts— watches, perfume bottles, needle cases, and fine lace. Wolfgang especially prized his shiny sword. When he wore it, he imagined he was the brave ruler of a kingdom of happy children. Sebastian Winter, who was the family's servant, drew a map of this imaginary kingdom for the boy. Wolfgang adored Sebastian's map. Imagining stories about the kingdom made the long rides seem to go by quickly.

The Mozarts' carriage reached the muddy streets of Paris in November. The city seemed a strange place. Everything appeared more richly decorated—the palaces, hotels, and coaches. Even the ladies decorated their faces with heavy makeup. In the middle of all this elegance, the streets were filled with muck. Wolfgang couldn't walk in them without getting dirty. So Papa hired sedan chairs. These boxes with seats inside were carried on two long poles. Wolfgang peered out with wide eyes at the busy city as he rode in a sedan chair.

At Christmas time, the Mozarts were invited to the royal court at the palace of Versailles. The palace was magnificent, but its huge halls were cold and damp. King Louis XV and his court marveled at the talented Mozart children. On New Year's Day, the royal family dined at a richly spread table. The Mozart family was invited to stand by the dinner table. It was the royals' way of showing their favor. The queen spoke to Wolfgang in German as she fed him morsels of food. Wolfgang thought she spoke German very well.

Wolfgang wrote an entry in his journal in French for Papa to read. While they traveled, Papa wanted Wolfgang and Nannerl to learn the language of each country they visited. He required them to write in their journals using the language of the country they were visiting. Without formal schooling, the world was Wolfgang's classroom, and Papa was his teacher. Wolfgang not only learned music but languages, literature, geography, history, mathematics, and manners.

In 1764 Wolfgang's first works were published. They were two sets of sonatas—music for a solo instrument with keyboard or orchestra accompaniment. The sonatas were dedicated to members of the royal court. Wolfgang was eight years old.

In April the Mozarts were on another boat, this time crossing the English Channel and bound for London. Wolfgang was seasick. Nannerl was seasick. Papa and Mama were seasick. But they all arrived safely in London. It wasn't long before Wolfgang and Nannerl received an invitation to perform for King George III and Queen Charlotte. The English royalty seemed to the Mozarts to be more down-to-earth than other royalty.

One day Wolfgang was walking in a London park when he heard laughter. He looked up to see King George leaning out of his carriage window, giving Wolfgang a friendly wave.

In London, Wolfgang was able to hear music he would have never heard at home—music by George Frideric Handel and the singing of Giovanni Manzuoli, the famous Italian singer. Though Wolfgang was only eight years old, older musicians spoke seriously with him. One of them was Johann Christian Bach, the son of the great composer Johann Sebastian Bach. Wolfgang sat at the organ with the younger Bach, taking turns playing. People who were listening said they couldn't tell when one left off playing and the other began. Bach enjoyed teaching Wolfgang, and of course, Wolfgang wanted to learn everything he could.

In London, people were used to attending public concerts, so the children gave many of them. Papa made posters advertising a concert. The posters called eight-year-old Wolfgang, "The greatest prodigy that Europe or that even Human Nature has to boast of."

In his concerts, Wolfgang sight-read music. He played music he had written. Then he and Nannerl played together on the harpsichord. They amazed the audience by covering the keyboard with a handkerchief and playing without seeing the keys.

When Papa was in bed with a severe cold, Wolfgang had to be quiet. To keep busy, he was writing his first symphony—a long piece of music for orchestra that was usually divided into three or four distinct movements. Nannerl sat beside Wolfgang to help copy it down. She reminded him to make sure there was something interesting for the horns to play.

Before leaving London in August 1765, Wolfgang also wrote his first work for chorus. *God Is Our Refuge* was a short anthem with words in English. His father presented it to the British Museum. Wolfgang was only nine years old, but he had already written four concertos—music for a solo instrument and orchestra. He also had written five symphonies and more than ten sonatas.

On their way home, the Mozarts made a detour through the Netherlands. Papa wanted to promote Wolfgang while he was still young enough to be a child marvel.

One damp October day in The Hague, Nannerl was feeling too sick to perform or even to write in her journal. In the next few days, she became so ill with fever that her parents thought she wouldn't live. After many fearful days and nights, she began to recover. But on November 15, Wolfgang began to feel ill. He had caught the same fever. For eight days, he was barely conscious. His lips were blackened, and he couldn't speak. The boy was very ill for weeks. But the family's prayers were answered, and he pulled through. His parents carried him from the bed to a chair. Slowly, Wolfgang grew strong enough to walk across the room.

Papa decided to delay travel until Wolfgang was completely well. By the end of January, the children were giving their first concert for a Dutch audience. Then they journeyed through France and Switzerland. Wolfgang became known throughout Europe as a wonder child. He was still a boy but also a remark-able young composer, full of promise.

3

Italian Journeys

Wolfgang felt the rhythm of the horses' hooves grow slower as the coach wheeled into Salzburg. He was home at last. It was December 1766, and he had been on the road for three and a half years.

Wolfgang let his thoughts wander as he listened to the song of his pet canary. Now that he was home again, much of his time was spent studying counterpoint—using two melodies at the same time in a composition. Wolfgang admired the way Handel had written counterpoint in his *Water Music.* But Herr Canary's songs always delighted Wolfgang too.

A year later, the Mozarts returned to Vienna. While they were there, Emperor Joseph II suggested that Wolfgang write an opera—a play where the words were sung and an orchestra accompanied the singers. Wolfgang wrote *La finta semplice,* which Papa thought very good. But some people did not believe Wolfgang had written the small comic opera himself. Some of the performers did not want to be directed by a twelve-year-old boy. To Wolfgang's great disappointment, the performance was called off.

Wolfgang wrote another small opera. *Bastien und Bastienne* was a story about two charming country folk. It was performed at the home of Dr. Franz Mesmer, a famous physician and hypnotist. Musical performances were often given at the homes of wealthy people who invited their friends.

Back at home and feeling strong again, Wolfgang enjoyed the admiration of Salzburg. His father's employer, the archbishop, asked him to compose music for the church. These melodic compositions began to show his true gift for writing music.

In December 1769, thirteen-year-old Wolfgang and his father were off to Italy. Nannerl and Mama waved good-bye. Wolfgang had promised to write to Nannerl about his adventures. He would miss his sister, who had always been his traveling companion and fellow performer. Who would he tease?

Italy was known for producing beautiful melodies, fine singers, and the best opera. Wolfgang and his father headed south to Milan, where Wolfgang performed at the home of a count. Leopold wrote home that the count was greatly impressed with Wolfgang's talent.

Wolfgang enjoyed his celebrity and was in high spirits. He wrote to tell his sister about the people he met. He was amused that the king of Naples stood on a little stool at the opera so that he would look taller than the queen. Wolfgang criticized one singer who sang well but not loud enough. "She cannot open her mouth, but whimpers everything," he wrote. He teased Nannerl. "A hundred little kisses or smacks on that wondrous horse-face of yours!" he wrote, using one of his favorite terms for her.

His letters were filled with fun and nonsense, but Wolfgang was on serious business. The arias—or songs—he wrote were so well received that he was asked to compose an opera. *Mitridate, rè di Ponto* would be performed during the holiday season in Milan the following December. So in the meantime, he had time for other things.

As father and son continued traveling south, Wolfgang wrote his first string quartet—music for two violins, a viola, and a cello. In Bologna, he met Padre Giovanni Martini, a famous composer and teacher. Wolfgang took some lessons in counterpoint from the grand old master. In Parma, Wolfgang heard a soprano sing impossibly high notes. He was so impressed that he wrote down the notes for Nannerl in his next letter.

Wolfgang and his father made their way to Rome. From a seat in the Sistine Chapel, Wolfgang studied the ceiling. There, more than two hundred years earlier, Michelangelo had painted a magnificent fresco of the creation of the world. When the service started, Wolfgang listened to the choir sing the sacred *Miserere,* written one hundred years before by Gregorio Allegri. By order of the pope, this music could only be sung in the Sistine Chapel. The choir members were not even allowed to take the music home. Wolfgang memorized the *Miserere* as he listened. When he returned to the inn, he sat down and wrote out all nine voice parts. Two days later, he tucked the papers into his hat and went back to the chapel to hear the music again. After he made a few small changes, Wolfgang's copy was entirely accurate.

Wolfgang was busy writing symphonies and church music during his year in Italy. He wrote to Nannerl complaining that his fingers ached from writing so much music. In October he returned to Milan to finish writing his opera *Mitridate* for the city's holiday celebration. Before the opera even went into rehearsals, some musicians tried to stop the performance. They were jealous of a fourteen-year-old boy and a foreigner writing an Italian opera. But once the rehearsals began, the singers and orchestra musicians realized Wolfgang had done a remarkable job. At the first performance on December 26, 1770, the audience loved it.

Wolfgang and Papa returned to Salzburg for several months, but they went back to Italy. Wolfgang had been asked to compose a theatrical work for the royal wedding of Archduke Ferdinand.

Wolfgang had only a month to write the music for *Ascanio in Alba* because the poet was slow in getting the words to him. But that was all he needed. He wrote home to Nannerl about the place where he and Papa were staying. "Above us is a violinist, beneath us is another, next to us is a singing teacher who gives lessons, and in the room opposite us is an oboe player. That is fun to compose by! It gives one plenty of ideas."

When *Ascanio in Alba* was performed during the wedding festivities, it was a huge success. His friend the great singer Giovanni Manzuoli sang one of the parts. *Ascanio* outshone a new opera by the composer Johann Adolph Hasse. Hasse generously declared to his fellow musicians, "This boy will throw us all in the shade." People stopped Wolfgang on the street to congratulate him.

Leopold had hoped the bridegroom, Archduke Ferdinand, would offer Wolfgang a job at the royal court. But the archduke's mother, Empress Maria Theresa, had advised against hiring Wolfgang. She had found him charming when he was a little boy. But she did not approve of his father toting him across Europe. She felt Leopold Mozart ignored his own duties to the archbishop in Salzburg.

When Wolfgang was sixteen, father and son made another trip to Italy. During this trip, Wolfgang composed another opera, *Lucio Silla.* The remarkable male soprano Venanzio Rauzzini helped to make this opera a success, and Wolfgang wanted to thank him. He sat at his writing desk and began putting down the music for a motet—a song for church. *Exsultate, jubilate* meant "exultation, jubilation." He created the joyful melodies, arching phrases, trills, jumps, and runs that Italian opera singers loved to sing. Wolfgang's brilliant motet showed the skill he had gained in the Italian song style. He knew it would fit Rauzzini's voice perfectly.

When he left Italy, Wolfgang was seventeen years old. He could no longer be called a wonder child, but his extraordinary genius had certainly grown.

4

Finding His Way

A little night music floated toward him on the evening air as Wolfgang made his way to the masquerade in the town hall. Now that his family had put down roots again, there was time for the teenager to enjoy the social life of Salzburg. Salzburg seemed small and unsophisticated after life in the great courts of Europe. But the family enjoyed get-togethers with good friends to play cards or throw horseshoes. Wolfgang liked attending plays, dances, and masked balls. He frequently made music with friends. Wolfgang also used his time to study languages and read literature. He could often be seen pulling a good book out of his pocket.

Salzburg was changing. The old Archbishop Schrattenbach had died, and Archbishop Colloredo took his place as head of state in Salzburg. He was Leopold's new employer.

Archbishop Colloredo gave Wolfgang a job as concertmaster. He was expected to compose and play music for the church and for court occasions. But the archbishop cut back on the amount of new music required. He sent for Italian musicians instead and paid them more. Colloredo was more interested in having Wolfgang perform than compose. So Wolfgang had time to write music for other wealthy patrons and friends. As a result, he became known as the top local composer.

In 1773 Wolfgang and his father went to Vienna. While Wolfgang was there, he heard plenty of new music. He was excited by the new string quartets of Joseph Haydn. Inspired by Haydn, Wolfgang wrote some string quartets. Returning to Salzburg, Wolfgang continued to use what he had learned from Haydn.

Mozart carried around a lively melody in his head. As he wrote his Symphony no. 29, he began with that lively melody. He repeated it again and again, but with changes each time. Then he ended the first movement—or section—by bringing back the original lively melody. In the second movement, he wrote soft, flowing music for the violins. Next came a minuet—a slow, lilting dance. Finally, he wrote a strong, spirited finale—the final movement. It was a symphony that expressed drama and deep emotion.

Wolfgang grew less and less satisfied working for Archbishop Colloredo. At twenty-one, he had never been on his own. He wanted to write operas, but there was little call for them in Salzburg. Opera was his favorite form. He could use the music to tell a story and show the characters. He loved working with singers. He also had a knack for writing songs that were perfect for each singer's voice and ability.

Wolfgang decided to go on tour. He began to polish his piano playing and wrote six piano sonatas to take with him on the road. The piano was a relatively new instrument. It had been invented by Bartolomeo Cristofori in 1710. Its early name, pianoforte, meant "soft-loud" in Italian. Unlike a clavier or harpsichord, a piano's dynamics could be controlled. Pressing softly made a softer sound. Pressing hard made a louder one. This gave Wolfgang more freedom to change the mood during a piece, and it added to the richness of the music.

When Wolfgang and Leopold asked Archbishop Colloredo for a leave of absence to go on tour, they were both fired. The archbishop would not put up with their traveling. Leopold apologized and was given his job back. Wolfgang was eager to go on tour alone, but his father would not allow it. Mama must go to make sure Wolfgang didn't get into trouble.

In Mannheim, Wolfgang made friends with other musicians, including Johann Cannabich. Wolfgang and his friends often enjoyed dinners that stretched into laughter late at night. His friends convinced Wolfgang that a job would soon open up at court in Mannheim. Yet he received no offer. After being the center of attention for most of his life, Wolfgang could be cocky, outspoken, and impatient. These traits did not help him earn a position at court.

One day, Johann Cannabich took Wolfgang to meet Fridolin Weber. Weber was a copyist—he wrote copies of music for the orchestra members. Weber had four daughters—Josepha, Aloisia, Constanze, and Sophie. Wolfgang heard Aloisia sing, and he fell in love. He wanted to help her singing career. He wrote to his father that he was considering marriage.

Leopold became furious and wrote back to remind his son of the hardships and costs of this trip. He told Wolfgang that he had an obligation to his family to find a responsible position. Wolfgang wanted to be independent, but his father would not let go. Leopold did not approve of Wolfgang's conduct or his friends. He ordered him on to Paris. Wolfgang felt he had no choice but to follow his father's command. Before leaving Mannheim, he wrote a lovely soprano aria, and Aloisia gave its first performance.

On March 14, Wolfgang and his mother left for Paris. They arrived nine days later in a driving rainstorm. Though a friend tried to open doors for Wolfgang, there was not much work for him in Paris. It had been easier for him to attract attention as a gifted child.

Wolfgang went to the grand home of the Countess de Chabot and was escorted inside. The stately room with its high ceilings was ice cold. There was not even a fireplace to warm his numb fingers. The countess greeted Wolfgang graciously. But while he played, the countess chatted with her friends. Wolfgang was insulted. He felt as if he were playing to the furniture.

At last he was asked to write a symphony. Paris would finally take note of him! The *Paris* Symphony was well received at its premiere in June. Walking back to his rooms in good spirits, Wolfgang treated himself to ice cream.

Wolfgang had to resort to teaching a few private students to earn money. He disliked teaching. It took time away from the creative work he loved—composing. He wrote a concerto for flute and harp, but he had trouble collecting his fee from the duke who had hired him. He was unhappy and pined for Aloisia.

Wolfgang returned to his lodgings one day in June to find his mother very ill. He knew traveling had been difficult for her. He had often left her alone. For several days, she grew sicker. Then Wolfgang sent for a priest. Mama died on the evening of July 3. Stricken with grief and guilt, Wolfgang sat down to write the terrible news to his father and sister.

Wolfgang felt lost. Should he stay in Paris in the hope of getting more work? Should he go back to Mannheim where he had been so happy? Should he travel to Munich where Aloisia was making a name for herself as a singer? Leopold wrote to him to come home to Salzburg. A position had opened up for Wolfgang as court organist.

Wolfgang made his way toward home, first stopping in Mannheim and Munich. It did his soul good to see his friends again. He had written a dramatic solo especially for Aloisia while he was in Paris. Wolfgang was eager to hear her sing it so he could put the finishing touches on it. At last, he saw Aloisia, but she snubbed him. She had become too successful to waste her time on a young composer.

In his letters, Leopold tried everything to get Wolfgang home again. When threats and scolding didn't work, he coaxed and made promises. Wolfgang finally arrived back in Salzburg six months after his mother's death. It had taken him that long to face his father again.

5

Freedom

In the distance, the post horn announced the arrival of the coach bringing mail to Salzburg. To Wolfgang, the trumpetlike sound was a reminder of far off places. He was not content playing the organ in the cathedral and writing music ordered by the archbishop. In spite of this, his compositions reached new levels of vivid expression. He composed two beautiful masses—music for the main church service. One was the grand and festive *Coronation* Mass and the other, the somber *Missa solemnis.* He also wrote music for evening vespers—an evening church service. In *Vesperae solennes de Confessore,* he wove together a four-part chorus and soloists. He arranged the music around the prayerful words to give them emphasis, tying the meaning and the music together.

Apart from music for the archbishop, Wolfgang wrote a good deal of instrumental music—concertos, sonatas, and symphonies. He also wrote the *Posthorn* Serenade. In it, he cleverly used the common post horn that he heard when the mail coach arrived.

In 1780 Wolfgang received a request to come to Munich and compose an opera for the winter carnival. The request lifted Wolfgang's spirits. The Mannheim Orchestra was in Munich then. His friends would be there. This was the opportunity he had been hoping for—to write an opera and work with an excellent orchestra. To Wolfgang's relief, Archbishop Colloredo gave him permission to go.

The small, pale, smartly dressed young man arrived in Munich carrying a satchel of music. Wolfgang was so full of ideas that he had begun writing *Idomeneo rè di Creta* before he left home. He used the fine orchestra to its best advantage. He made the musicians work hard, and he praised them. He rewrote some of the singers' parts to fit their voices.

The opera was a solid success, and Papa and Nannerl were there to see its premiere. Wolfgang stayed in Munich for a while to bask in his triumph. It wasn't long before Archbishop Colloredo decided to spend some time in Vienna, and he commanded Wolfgang to join him there.

Vienna! Mozart parted from his father and sister and set out to make a new life for himself in a city he loved. He wanted never again to be subject to his father's authority. The Weber family had moved to Vienna, and Fridolin had died not long after. Though Aloisia had married an actor named Joseph Lange, Wolfgang was still on friendly terms with her and her family.

In Vienna at Archbishop Colloredo's court, Wolfgang was given a servant's room. Wolfgang certainly did not see himself as a mere servant. He grumbled in his letters to Papa that he had to sit at the long dinner table next to the cooks. He was made to wear the red livery worn by all members of the orchestra. Wolfgang bristled at being treated this way—he was a gifted composer.

Once when they were to play at a royal palace, he refused to march into the music room with the orchestra. Instead, he strode in alone. Wolfgang walked straight up to a prince he knew and greeted him, with no regard for formalities.

As part of his duties, Wolfgang was expected to wait in the corridor every morning in case the archbishop wanted to speak to him. Wolfgang was too busy setting up his own private appearances with important people to do that. He knew it was just a matter of time before he would resign. But the archbishop didn't wait for him. Colloredo ordered Wolfgang to pack up and leave. Wolfgang threw his things into his trunk and went to stay with his friends the Webers.

In the following weeks, Wolfgang tried to see the archbishop again. The archbishop's assistant refused to let him in. He called Wolfgang a clown and a knave. Then he grabbed Wolfgang and threw him out the door with a kick. Wolfgang was finished.

He was furious. But his anger soon gave way, and he began to take a brighter view of his situation. He felt that his run of luck was just beginning. Wolfgang was finally free of ties to Salzburg. Mama Weber and her daughters fed and comforted him. They took good care of him for a few weeks until he found rooms of his own. Wolfgang began to notice that Aloisia's younger sister Constanze had sparkling black eyes.

Wolfgang wasted no time after being fired by the archbishop. He gave more concerts, both private and public. By the end of 1781, he was known as the best keyboard player in Vienna. Emperor Joseph II arranged for a contest between Wolfgang Mozart and Muzio Clementi. Clementi was an Italian composer and pianist. Wolfgang won the contest, but he was surprised when Clementi proved to be stiff competition. Wolfgang also published five sonatas for piano and violin. One reviewer called them "rich in new ideas and traces of their author's great musical genius."

Emperor Joseph II was impressed with Wolfgang Mozart's work and asked him to write an opera for a royal visit by Grand Duke Paul, son of Catherine the Great. As Wolfgang began writing *The Abduction from the Seraglio,* the ideas poured from his pen. The heroine of this opera was named Constanze, and the story told how goodness led to happiness. Wolfgang crafted a different kind of opera—the music helped create the characters. Listeners could tell by the music if a character was good or evil, jealous, frightened, or loving.

Wolfgang explained to his father how he wrote one of the arias. He used the violins to express a throbbing heart. He made the music swell to show a heart swelling with love. He used softer violins with a flute so listeners would hear whispering and sighing. Wolfgang had masterfully used the music to show the feelings and actions of the characters.

The Abduction from the Seraglio was a big success. It was performed in July of 1782, with Wolfgang conducting the orchestra from his keyboard. The opera had great popular appeal, and the theater was packed for every performance. The emperor approved.

At twenty-five, Wolfgang found himself longing to settle down. Constanze was nineteen years old, a pleasant girl and easy to talk with. She had a tender way about her that made him feel good when he was with her. She had a lovely singing voice. Wolfgang and Constanze enjoyed laughing and singing together. They loved each other. Wolfgang thought someone as good-natured and fun-loving as Constanze would make a good wife and mother.

Out of respect for his father, Wolfgang wrote to ask for his consent to the marriage. Leopold wrote back telling Wolfgang he would not give his permission. On August 4, 1782, however, the confident young composer married Constanze Weber, the young woman he loved. It was just two weeks after the success of his new opera. Leopold could no longer control Wolfgang's life.

The next June, Wolfgang worked on the string quartets he planned to dedicate to his respected friend, the famous composer Joseph Haydn. And Constanze gave birth to their first son. Leopold did not come to the baptism of his first grandchild. Sadly, little Raimund Leopold only lived until August.

Wolfgang took Constanze to Salzburg, so that Papa and Nannerl could meet her. He hoped they would accept her as one of the family. It hurt him deeply when Leopold and Nannerl were cold to her. Constanze sang Wolfgang's unfinished Mass in C minor in St. Peter's Church. Before leaving for home, Constanze asked Leopold if she could select a memento from among the gifts Wolfgang had earned as a child. Leopold refused to let her have even one. The young couple turned their backs on Salzburg and went home.

6

The Magic Pen

Wolfgang Mozart strolled through the square, past the spires of St. Stephen's cathedral, humming to himself. His after-dinner walk through the park had given him a chance to think. In truth, he was composing. He had been working on a musical idea, turning it over in his mind as if he were in a waking dream. The music fired his soul. He heard the instruments and worked out the counterpoint. He was able to survey all of it at once, as if he were glancing at a fine painting. As Mozart turned the corner toward home again, he filed away the music in his memory. Later, he would write it all down.

These were happy and busy times for Mozart. He wrote for concerts that he organized and then performed in. He wrote for his friends who gathered to play quartets in his home. Though he didn't have a court position, he was able to support himself and Constanze. In one month, he scheduled and performed in twenty-one concerts of his own music.

Mozart chuckled to himself. He was finishing a horn concerto for his good friend Joseph Leutgeb, who was a horn player. Feeling mischievous, he wanted to write a passage that would be almost impossible to play. Mozart wrote it in bright blue ink. Then in the margin he scribbled, "Ha! What do you say to that, Master Leutgeb?"

Mozart began keeping a list of his works, writing the date by each one. In less than two year's time, he had listed a dozen piano concertos. Mozart was so busy that sometimes he was late getting the notes down on paper for the musicians. He wrote a brilliant sonata for piano and violin to play with Regina Strinasacchi, a violinist. Poor Regina had to perform it without a rehearsal. Mozart barely had time to write out her part. He performed his piano part with blank sheets of paper in front of him. Amazingly, he had memorized the music before he had even written it down. He did the same once when he played with a group for Emperor Joseph II. But the emperor caught Mozart at his trick. He looked through his opera glasses and saw the blank pages. Mozart assured the emperor afterward that "not a single note was lost!"

Nannerl was married on August 23, 1784, near Salzburg. Wolfgang did not travel to the wedding—he fell ill with fever that day.

He was feeling better by the time his second son, Karl Thomas, was born on September 21, 1784. The Mozarts were thankful their little son was strong. They needed more room for the baby and for the servants, cook, hairdressers, copyists, and musicians who came and went in their busy household. So they moved to a larger apartment. In January, Mozart quickly dashed off some dancing music to pay the bills.

Mozart's fame was growing. He regularly invited friends to his home for Sunday morning concerts. He wrote to his father to let him know that things were going well. Nannerl was living on her husband's estate, and Leopold was alone and lonely. Leopold finally came to visit his son in Vienna in February of 1785. Wolfgang gave a party to present his six string quartets to Joseph Haydn. Haydn told Leopold, "Your son is the greatest composer known to me."

Mozart's new pet starling delighted him. He had found a songbird that could sing the theme from his Piano Concerto no. 17 in G, almost note for note. Mozart recorded the price of the starling in his account book. Then he wrote the notes of the song and the comment, "That was lovely."

Though Mozart was considered the greatest pianist in Vienna, he still had no steady job with the court. He wanted a chance to write another opera. Antonio Salieri was the powerful kapellmeister at court. Mozart worried that Salieri and other court musicians were working against him out of jealousy.

At a party one evening, Mozart was introduced to a tall man with striking looks and long dark hair. He was Lorenzo Da Ponte, a new court poet. Da Ponte wanted to write an opera, and Mozart had a play in mind called *The Marriage of Figaro*. Da Ponte read the story and wanted to start work on it right away. For six weeks, Mozart wrote the music as fast as Da Ponte could get the words to him. When Da Ponte went to Emperor Joseph II, he agreed to listen to it. And when the emperor heard Mozart play the wonderful music, he ordered the performance.

At the first orchestra rehearsal of *The Marriage of Figaro,* the entire orchestra rose to their feet, clapping. Grasping his long crimson cloak with one hand and removing his gold-laced hat with the other, Mozart bowed deeply to show his gratitude.

At the premiere on May 1, 1786, *Figaro* was a triumph. The audience demanded to hear almost every piece of music a second time. Mozart had developed his ability to paint the characters with music. In

Figaro, the characters were real human beings, and the arias they sang showed their moods.

Mozart and Constanze received an invitation from the orchestra and music society in Prague. When they went to Prague in January 1787, Mozart found the whole city was *Figaro*-crazy. "They play, they sing, they whistle nothing but—*Figaro!*" he wrote to his father. Mozart and Constanze enjoyed a month of good times in Prague. They attended balls where every dance seemed to be taken from the melodies of *Figaro.* Mozart conducted his opera for a wildly enthusiastic audience. Though his music was popular, Mozart didn't earn a penny from all these performances. Composers were only paid for their work when it was first performed.

Mozart also gave a concert of his new Symphony no. 38. Audiences loved it, and it became known as the *Prague* Symphony. Before he left Prague, Mozart agreed to write an opera to be given the next year.

Wolfgang and Constanze moved again, this time to a quiet place outside Vienna. It had a beautiful garden where Wolfgang could hear the birds sing while he worked. Their third son, Johann Thomas Leopold, born in the fall, had only lived a few weeks. Wolfgang worried about Constanze's health. She made visits to the spa at Baden, about fifteen miles away. The trips were costly, but the sulfur-spring baths there seemed to help her.

It was a heavy blow when Wolfgang received word in May 1787 that his father had died. Later, he learned that Leopold left all his savings to Nannerl, even the earnings from Wolfgang's childhood tours. Wolfgang asked Nannerl to return all his manuscripts to him. After he received them, he stopped writing to his sister.

The summer after Leopold's death, Mozart and Lorenzo Da Ponte started work on the new opera, *Don Giovanni*. It had to be ready to take to Prague in October. As they worked throughout the summer, Mozart took a break now and then to write instrumental music. In August he penned *A Little Night Music*. He gave this touching serenade moments of true beauty and grace.

Wolfgang and Constanze set out on their second trip to Prague in early October for the opening of *Don Giovanni*. Mozart had written the overture—the musical introduction—just days before. The audience cheered as the composer took his place at the keyboard to conduct the orchestra. The fast pace of the music kept the action moving on stage, and the melodies fit the characters perfectly. Mozart seemed to have gathered up all the powerful emotions he felt at his father's death and put them into this towering masterpiece. *Don Giovanni* proved to be an even greater achievement than his earlier operas.

As Mozart was returning to Vienna in November 1787, the esteemed court composer Christoph Gluck died. In December, Mozart was at last honored with an official position. Emperor Joseph II named him imperial court composer. His salary was less than half of what Gluck had received, but it would help with his debts. His duties would only require him to write dances for the court balls once a year. No matter, Mozart finally had the recognition and respect he felt he deserved as a composer.

The family moved back into the city of Vienna. Constanze gave birth to a girl, Theresia Constanzia, in December. However, their little daughter only survived six months. Although Mozart's family lived comfortably, at times he struggled to pay the bills and had to borrow from friends. To pay some debts during the summer of 1788, he began writing music for a series of concerts. In six short weeks, he created three remarkable symphonies. The third one, Symphony no. 41, was one of his greatest achievements. In it, Mozart demonstrated brilliant musical technique and powerful emotional expression. It came to be called the *Jupiter* Symphony.

By 1791 Mozart felt he was realizing his dreams. He was court composer, and he had operas to write. His career and finances were looking brighter. He was working night and day to keep up. He completed the beautiful Piano Concerto no. 27 to play at a benefit concert. He was commissioned to write an opera for the coronation celebration of Leopold II in Prague.

Busy though he was, Mozart took time out to write a motet for his friend Anton Stoll, the director of a small choir. Mozart wrote the masterful *Ave verum corpus* for Stoll's choir to sing on a church feast day. Its simple, direct style conveyed deep devotion.

A new idea fired Mozart's imagination. His friend Emanuel Schikaneder had asked him to write a "magic opera" for his theater company. Schikaneder was the owner of a popular theater. His troupe performed light comic opera called singspiel. These operas were partly spoken in German and partly sung. They were entertainment for the common people as well as the upper class.

Mozart and Schikaneder created a story that represented a journey of the soul. Mozart wrote playful folklike melodies, soaring arias, and exalted choruses. It was a magical work indeed. On September 30, Mozart conducted the opening of *The Magic Flute*. His German opera was hugely popular.

While Mozart was writing *The Magic Flute,* Franz Xaver was born. Wolfgang and Constanze rejoiced that their sixth child was healthy.

One day a messenger brought Mozart an unusual request to write a requiem—a mass for the dead. Count Walsegg-Stuppach commissioned it to honor his wife who had died. But the count wanted Mozart to leave his name off of the Requiem so that the count could pass it off as his own work!

Mozart began to work on this Requiem. He created bold and expressive harmonies. Like the master that he was, he skillfully mixed the styles of church and opera.

At the end of November, Mozart became seriously ill. The doctors could do very little to help him. For days he suffered, unable to leave his bed. Constanze could only pray that he would recover.

Mozart was only thirty-five years old when he died in the very early hours of December 5, 1791. He never finished his Requiem. He had completed some parts and had sketches for the others.

Wolfgang Amadeus Mozart had no grand funeral. He was buried according to the custom of the time in a simple grave. There was no graveside ceremony. There was not even a grave marker. His wondrous music would be his monument.

Afterword

No one is certain of the exact place where Mozart was buried. After his death, Constanze had Mozart's assistant finish the Requiem using Mozart's sketches. Music scholars still study the Requiem and puzzle over which parts Mozart truly wrote.

Mozart's two sons, Karl Thomas and Franz Xaver, grew to adulthood. Neither son married nor had children. Constanze married again, and her second husband helped her publish a biography of Mozart.

In 1862 Ludwig von Köchel printed a catalog listing of Mozart's works to more clearly identify them. As best as he could, he numbered the works in the order they were written. That is why the titles of Mozart's works today have a "K number" after them. The "K" stands for Köchel.

Without a doubt, Mozart was a towering musical genius and one of the greatest composers that music has ever known. He wrote with mastery in every musical form of his time. He combined extraordinary genius with serious study and almost constant work. He produced a huge volume of immortal works in his short lifetime. Many scholars have been challenged to sort out the facts from the myths that arose after his death. The final truth lies in his music. Listen to it for the whole story.

Selected Works

Here are Mozart's works that are referred to in the text. (K. refers to Köchel number.)

Operas

Bastien und Bastienne (K. 50)	1768
La finta semplice (K. 51)	1768
Mitridate, rè di Ponto (K. 87)	1770
Ascanio in Alba (K. 111)	1771
Lucio Silla (K. 135)	1772
Idomeneo, rè di Creta (K. 366)	1780-81
The Abduction from the Seraglio (K. 384)	1781-82
The Marriage of Figaro (K. 492)	1785–86
Don Giovanni (K. 527)	1787
The Magic Flute (K. 620)	1791

Aria

Alcandro, lo confesso (K. 294)	1778

Church Music

God Is Our Refuge (K. 20)	1765
Missa brevis (K. 65)	1769
Exsultate, jubilate (K. 165)	1773
Mass in C; *Coronation* (K. 317)	1779
Mass in C minor (K. 427)	1782–83
Missa solemnis (K. 337)	1780
Vesperae solennes de confessore (K. 339)	1780
Ave verum corpus (K. 618)	1791
Requiem in D (K. 626)	1791

Symphonies

No. 1 (K. 16)	1764
No. 29 (K. 201)	1774
No. 31; *Paris* (K. 297)	1778
No. 38; *Prague* (K. 504)	1786
No. 41; *Jupiter* (K. 551)	1788

Concertos

Flute and Harp (K. 299)	1778
Horn no. 2 (K. 417)	1783
Piano no. 17 (K. 453)	1784
Piano no. 27 (K. 595)	1791

Violin Sonatas

C major (K. 6)	1764
D major (K. 7)	1764
B flat major (K. 8)	1764
G major (K. 9)	1764
C major (K. 296)	1778
F major (K. 376)	1781
F major (K. 377)	1781
G major (K. 379)	1781
E flat major (K. 380)	1781
B flat major; *Strinasacchi* (K. 454)	1784

Piano Sonatas

C major (K. 279)	1774
F major (K. 280)	1774
B flat major (K. 281)	1774
E flat major (K. 282)	1774
G major (K. 283)	1774
D major; *Durnitz* (K. 284)	1775

String Quartets

No. 2 (K. 155)	1772
No. 3 (K. 156)	1772
No. 4 (K. 157)	1772–73
No. 5 (K. 158)	1773
No. 6 (K. 159)	1773
No. 7 (K. 160)	1773
No. 14 (K. 387)	1782
No. 15 (K. 421)	1783
No. 16 (K. 428)	1783
No. 17; *Hunt* (K. 458)	1784
No. 18 (K. 464)	1785
No. 19; *Dissonant* (K. 465)	1785

Other Instrumental Music

Serenade no. 9; *Posthorn* (K. 320)	1779
A Little Night Music (K. 525)	1787

Selected Bibliography

Davenport, Marcia. *Mozart.* New York: Charles Scribner's Sons, 1932.

Eisen, Cliff, and Stanley Sadie, eds. *The New Grove Mozart.* London: Macmillan, 2002

Gay, Peter. *Mozart.* New York: Penguin Putnam, 1999.

Gutman, Robert W. *Mozart: A Cultural Biography.* New York: Harcourt Brace & Company, 1999.

Kupferberg, Herbert. *Amadeus: A Mozart Mosaic.* New York: McGraw-Hill, 1986.

Landon, H. C. Robbins. *1791: Mozart's Last Year.* New York: Schirmer Books, 1988.

Monjo, F. N. *Letters to Horseface: Being the Story of Wolfgang Amadeus Mozart's Journey to Italy, 1769–1770, When He Was a Boy of Fourteen.* New York: Viking Press, 1975.

Mozart, Wolfgang Amadeus. *Mozart: The Man and the Artist Revealed in His Own Words.* Compiled by Friedrich Kerst. Translated by Henry Edward Krehbiel. New York: Dover Publications, 1965.

Parouty, Michel. *Mozart: From Child Prodigy to Tragic Hero.* Translated by Celia Skrine. New York: Harry N. Abrams, 1993.

Solomon, Maynard. *Mozart: A Life.* New York: HarperCollins, 1995.

Index

arias, 27, 36, 54, 58, 61

Bach, Johann Christian, 20

choral music, 22, 29, 36, 40.
See also church music
church music, 8, 26, 29, 59, 61:
Ave verum corpus, 58, 61;
Coronation Mass, 40, 61;
Exultate, jubilate, 31, 61;
Mass in C minor, 48, 61;
Missa solemnis, 40, 61;
Requiem, 59–60, 61;
*Vesperae solennes de
Confessore,* 40, 61
Clementi, Muzio, 44–45
Colloredo, Archbishop, 33–35,
41, 44
concertos, 9–10, 22, 41, 50, 52,
58, 61
counterpoint, 25, 27, 49

Da Ponte, Lorenzo, 53, 55

Ferdinand, Archduke, 30–31
flute, 38, 45, 61

Handel, George Frideric, 20, 25
harp, 38, 61
Haydn, Joseph, 34, 47, 52
Holy Roman Empire, 7, 8, 14, 17
horn, 22, 50, 61

instrumental music: *A Little
Night Music,* 55, 61;
Posthorn Serenade, 41, 61

Italy, 26–31

Joseph II, Emperor, 25, 44–45,
50, 53, 56

keyboard, 7–10, 14, 16, 19, 22,
44, 45. *See also* piano

London, England, 20–22

Manzuoli, Giovanni, 20, 30
Maria Theresa, Empress, 13–14,
16, 31
minuets, 34
motets, 22, 31
Mozart, Anna Maria, 7–9, 10,
20, 26, 35, 38–39
Mozart, Karl Thomas, 52, 60
Mozart, Constanze, 36, 44, 47,
50, 54–56, 59–60
Mozart, Franz Xaver Wolfgang,
59, 60
Mozart, Leopold, 7–10, 13,
16–23, 25–31, 33–35, 39, 41,
43, 47–48, 52, 55
Mozart, Maria Anna "Nannerl,"
7, 9, 10, 12, 14–23, 26–28,
41, 47–48, 52, 55
Mozart, Wolfgang Amadeus:
birth, 7–8; childhood, 7–31;
composing, 9–10, 22, 25–27,
33–35, 40–41, 45, 49–50, 52,
55–56, 58–59; death, 59; performing, 13, 14–18, 20–23,
38, 44, 50, 53; sight-reading,
16, 22; teaching, 38

63

About the Author

Barbara Allman writes for children and teachers. She has studied piano, voice, and dance. Her other books include *Dance of the Swan: A Story about Anna Pavlova* and *Her Piano Sang: A Story about Clara Schumann.*